Celebrating Jesus!

Christine Steiner
Illustrations by Children of God

published by
Fox Tales Children's Books

a division of
Our Written Lives, LLC
in San Antonio, Texas

www.OurWrittenLives.com

Copyright ©2020 Christine Steiner

steinerbooks.wordpress.com

Library of Congress Cataloging-in-Publication Data
Steiner, Christine
Celebrating Jesus!

Library of Congress Control Number: 2020905124
ISBN: 978-1-942923-43-5 (paperback)
ISBN: 978-1-942923-42-8 (hardback)

Unless otherwise noted, Scriptures are from the King James Version, public domain.

Cover by Emily Evans
"Christine Steiner and Sister, Kim Cemer, as Children."
The sisters received the Holy Ghost on the same day—April 23, 1973.

"Jesus and the Children" by Emily Evans, Lincoln, NE
Dedicated to LeRoy and Ruby Jones and Stuart Evans

Dedication

For my mother,
who was also my Sunday school teacher,
thank you.

For my children:
Adrienne, Ashley, Amber, and Alicia.

For my grandchildren:
Temperance and little Kurt.
I'm honored to be your Neena.

For my husband Tim, of 36 years,
the Daddy and Papa of our children.

For a special boy, who I needed in my life
to show me how much Jesus loves the little
children, Stephen Steiner.

For all the children who helped draw the
illustrations for this book. You have made this
book look good!

Introduction

I heard in Your Word that we are to teach children about the Lord. You are our God, the Lord alone. You are one. I am to love You alone. When I lay down my head and when I rise to start my day, I am to learn of all Your ways.

So, take me back to the beginning—to a world You made before I was born. Where the heavens declare Your glory and the earth Your handiwork.

From the ground, You made the first mom and dad. You breathed life into them. From the woman's womb, children were born, and from her seed came the promised Holy One.

From the very beginning, I was a part of Your plan. I came from a mom and a dad, to live in a world that belongs to You. It is a world You made, Heavenly Father. You had me in mind, and You call me to come and sit by Your side.

The Beginning

God sat me down to learn about the first man, Adam, and his lovely wife, Eve. He formed Adam from the dust of the ground. From Adam's rib, God made Eve. He created them in His image and likeness and placed them in a garden He made especially for them. God blessed them and told them to have children, take care of the garden, and rule over every living thing.

He planted herbs and fruit trees of different kinds to feed the new couple. It was a complete buffet line. God told the them about two special trees. The first, the tree of life, was a tree they could eat of, so they would never die. The second was the tree of the knowledge of good and evil. Of this tree, they must not eat because the day they do, they would surely die!

Adam and Eve were looking at the forbidden tree and came upon a snake hiding in the leaves. The snake spoke to Eve, and said, "Did God really say you must not eat from any tree in the garden?"

The woman replied, "We may eat fruit from the trees in the garden, but God did say, 'You must not eat fruit from the tree that is in the middle of the garden. You must not touch it, or you will die.'"

"Eden" by Ava Wasmundt, 10 years old, Mesa, AZ
Dedicated to Rev. Andrew & Sis. Shirley Wasmundt

The snake said to the woman, "You certainly will not die! God knows that when you eat from it, your eyes will be opened and you will be like Him, knowing good and evil."

Eve looked at the fruit that was on the tree and saw how good it looked and how pleasing it was to her eyes. She desired the wisdom it would give her, so she took a piece of fruit from the tree and ate it. She gave some to her husband, and he also ate it.

Then, something happened. Their minds were opened to knowledge, but it was not what they expected. They saw they were naked and were ashamed. They took fig leaves and hurriedly weaved them together to cover their nakedness.

Adam and his wife heard the voice of the Lord as He was walking in the garden in the cool of the day. They ran into the trees to hide from Him because they were naked and afraid.

God called to Adam, "Where are you?"

Adam answered, "I heard You coming, so I ran and hid, because I am naked and full of fear."

The Lord God said, "Who told you, you were naked? Have you eaten from the tree that I commanded you not to eat from?"

Adam said, "The woman You gave to me, she gave me some fruit, and I ate it."

The Lord God turned to the woman and said, "What have you done?"

Eve said, "The snake deceived me, so I ate it."

Then God cursed Adam, Eve, and the snake for what they had done. Now they could no longer live in the garden He made but would live in a world full of sin and shame.

Thankfully, God didn't send them out completely cursed, alone, and afraid. He gave them a promise to comfort their pain. He would raise up a man through the woman. The man would destroy the devil who brought sin and shame into the world.

Through Adam, sin entered the world God made and brought death to the whole human race. But God would bring a second Adam who would give us grace and everlasting life. He promised to make us a new home in the sky where we will live forever and never die.

Moses

As I sat and listened to God's Word, He told me of a Hebrew boy of the tribe of Levi. The boy's mother hid him for three months from the king of Egypt, who was called Pharaoh. Pharaoh wanted to toss all of the baby boys into the river to die, but God had a different plan for the one special Hebrew baby.

When his mother could no longer keep him hidden, she weaved a little basket and placed the child in it. She put it among the reeds along the bank of the Nile, and Mariam, his sister, kept an eye on her baby brother.

As Pharaoh's daughter went down to the Nile to take her morning bath, she saw the little basket floating in the water. She called to one of her maidens to fetch the basket and saw it was a Hebrew baby. She felt sorry for him and decided to keep him as her own son. She named him Moses, saying, "Because I drew him from the water."

Mariam went over to Pharaoh's daughter and told her she knew of a Hebrew woman who could nurse the baby for her. She told Mariam to go get her, and Mariam brought back their mother! When the child was old enough, his mother took him

"Moses" by Kennedy White, 11 years old
Landmark Apostolic Church, Juneau, AK

back to Pharaoh's daughter and the little boy became her son.

One day, after Moses was grown up, he went out to where the Israelites were and saw the hard labor they did for Pharaoh. Moses saw an Egyptian beating a Hebrew man, and he became angry at what he saw. He was so angry; Moses killed the Egyptian and hid him in the sand. When Pharaoh heard about what happened, he came after Moses to kill him. So, Moses fled from Pharaoh and went to the land of Midian.

Moses met the priest of Midian and married the man's daughter, Zipporah. One day, while Moses was watching his father-in-law's sheep, he led the sheep to a place called Horeb, which means the mountain of God. In Horeb, Moses saw a burning bush. He went to get a closer look because he noticed the bush wasn't burning up in the fire.

God called Moses' name from the middle of the burning bush and told him He had seen the misery of His people. God wanted Moses to go to Egypt and deliver His people from the new Pharaoh.

Moses was afraid, and said to God, "Who am I that I should go to Pharaoh and bring the Israelites out of Egypt? If I go to the Israelites and say to them, 'The God of your fathers has sent me to you,' and they ask me, 'What is His name?' Then what shall I tell them?"

God answered Moses' question. "I AM WHO I AM. Tell the Israelites, I AM has sent me to you. I AM is My name forever, the name you shall call Me from generation to generation."

Moses and his brother, Aaron, went to Pharaoh and told him what God had said. Pharaoh responded, "Who is the Lord that I should obey him and let these people go? I do not know the LORD, and I will not let Israel go." After that, Pharaoh treated the Israelites even worse than he did before.

God said to Moses, "I AM the LORD. I appeared to Abraham, to Isaac, and to Jacob as God Almighty, but I did not make myself fully known to them by name. I established my covenant with them to give them the land of Canaan, where they resided as foreigners. I have heard the groaning of the Israelites, in slavery in Egypt, and I have remembered my covenant.

"Say to the Israelites My words: 'I AM, the LORD. I will bring you out from under the yoke of the Egyptians. I will free you from being slaves to them, and I will redeem you with an outstretched arm and with mighty acts of judgment. I will take you as My own people, and I will be your God. Then you will know that I AM the LORD your God who brought you out from under the yoke of the Egyptians. I will bring you to the land I swore to give to Abraham, to Isaac, and to Jacob. I will give it to you as a possession. I AM the LORD!'"

Moses performed wondrous miracles in Egypt, but Pharaoh's heart was hard against God. Then, God sent a total of ten plagues to curse Egypt. After each one, Pharaoh could have relented and let the children of Israel go, but he did not. It was time for the last and most devastating plague.

Moses told Pharaoh, "This is what the LORD said to me. 'About midnight, I will go throughout Egypt. Every firstborn son in Egypt will die from the firstborn son of Pharaoh, who sits on the throne, to the firstborn son of the female slave, who is at her hand mill, and all the firstborn of the cattle as well. There will be loud wailing throughout Egypt, worse than there has ever been or ever will be again.'"

The LORD also told Moses what to say to the community of Israel. "On the tenth day of this month, each man is to take a lamb for his family and slaughter the lamb as a sacrifice at twilight. You are to take some of the blood of the lamb and put it on the sides and tops of the door frames of your houses. Quickly eat the lambs, as if you are in a hurry to leave.

"You will remember this night as the LORD's Passover. This same night, I AM will pass through Egypt and strike down every firstborn of both people and animals and will bring judgment on all the gods of Egypt.

"The blood on your houses will be a sign. When the angel of the Lord sees the blood, he will pass over you, and your sons will not die. No destructive plague will touch you when He strikes Egypt."

At midnight, the LORD killed all the firstborn in Egypt, from the firstborn of Pharaoh, who sat on the throne, to the firstborn of the prisoner, who was in the dungeon, and the firstborn of all the livestock as well. Pharaoh, and all his officials, got up during the night. There was loud wailing in Egypt for there was not a house without someone dead. He was so distraught, Pharaoh let the people go.

Moses led the Israelites out of Egypt, and they all marched toward the Red Sea. God told Moses to raise his staff and stretch out his hand to divide the water of the sea. The waters divided, and the Israelites walked through the sea on dry ground. There was a wall of water on their right and on their left.

God was with them in the form of a cloud by day and a fire by night. He stood behind the children of Israel as they moved forward. After the people of God left Egypt, Pharaoh became angry, and he led his army after them to bring them back into slavery. God's cloud blocked light from Pharaoh and his army and shielded God's people. Neither one went near the other all night long.

Eventually, God allowed the Egyptians to arrive at the Red Sea. All of Pharaoh's horses, chariots, and soldiers followed God's people through the dry land where the sea had parted.

The Israelites made it to the other side, but the Egyptians were in the middle of the dry sea. God told Moses to let down his hand, and the water of the sea flowed back where it always had been, drowning the Egyptians. Pharaoh and his entire army were gone.

That day, the LORD saved Israel from the hand of the Egyptians. When the people saw the mighty hand of the LORD fighting for them against the Egyptians, the people feared the LORD and put their trust in Him. They followed Moses as their leader, God's servant.

After that day, Moses continued to lead God's people toward the Promised Land. They made many mistakes and had many lessons to learn. God would give them Commandments and a law to obey. Having a written law would help the people know God's ways, so they could strive to serve Him.

Moses told God's people, "The LORD God will fulfill the promise He made to Abraham, Isaac, and Jacob to give them an inheritance. He has given us His Holy Law to obey as we enter the Promised Land. The Lord your God, He is one! And, you are to love Him with all your heart, soul, and strength. Keep all the words the Lord commands in your hearts, so you can teach them diligently to your children!"

The people went into an agreement with God and promised to obey, but they soon broke their covenant with Him. They served other gods and disobeyed God's law. They spent many years repenting and turning back to God, and then sinning and turning away from Him again.

Many years later, God spoke through the prophet Jeremiah and gave His people a promise of what was to come. He would make a new covenant with the house of Israel. God would put His law in their minds and write it on their hearts. Then, the Israelites would be His people and He would be their God. God promised to forgive their iniquity and sin, and to remember it no more.

The new covenant would bring forgiveness of sins, but forgiveness could not come from the blood of animals. Forgiveness and remission of sin required the blood of a sinless sacrifice. The sacrifice would be from a Passover Lamb that would be without spot or blemish. The Lamb would come from God and would be slain for the sins of the whole world.

The blood of the Lamb, when applied to the door post of the hearts of mankind, would set them free from the law of sin and death. As it happened that night in Egypt, when God saw the blood of the lamb on the door frames, He spared the people of that house. Now, the people would have the blood of the Lamb of God cover their souls. Because of the blood of the new covenant, people could have everlasting life and an inheritance in Heaven.

David

As I sat listening to God's Word, He told me about a boy named David who could pray and sing. The Lord told me how He sent the prophet Samuel to anoint David to be the king of His people. God told Samuel to take anointing oil, go to Bethlehem, and find a man named Jesse who had many sons.

"I have chosen one of them for you to anoint. He is the one I have chosen to be the king of Israel," the Lord said to Samuel. So, Samuel went to Bethlehem where he found the man and his sons. Then they all went with Samuel to sacrifice to the Lord.

Samuel looked at Jesse's oldest son Eliab. He thought to himself, "Surely, he's the one the Lord wants me to anoint as king!"

But God told Samuel, "He is not the one. You are looking at his outward appearance, but I'm looking at his heart."

Jesse showed Abinadab, Shammah, and five of his other sons to Samuel, but they were not the one God chose to be the king of Israel.

Samuel asked, "Are these the only sons you have?"

"No," Jesse answered, "I have a young shepherd boy who is in the field watching over the sheep."

Samuel said, "Send for him. I will not eat until I see him!"

David came from the field and stood before Samuel. He had a fair complexion, bright beautiful eyes, and was very nice looking.

The Lord spoke to Samuel saying, "Get up and anoint David with oil for he is the one I have chosen to be the king of Israel." The Spirit of the Lord came upon David from that day forward.

Before God's people acknowledged David as king, God sent him into battle. The children of Israel faced a Philistine army and a 9-foot giant. They were so afraid of the Philistine giant; they ran away shaking in their shoes.

David took his shepherd's sling and went to a nearby brook to pick out five smooth stones. Then, he returned to the battlefield and looked Goliath straight in the eyes. He shouted, "You come against me with your sword, javelin, and spear, but I come against you in the name of the Lord of hosts, the God of Israel."

As David ran toward Goliath, he slung his sling and sent one of the smooth stones flying into the air. The stone hit Goliath in the forehead, and the giant came tumbling down! When the Philistines saw their champion was dead and their enemy

"David" by LilieAnna Us, 12 years old
Battlefield Apostolic Church, Springfield, MO
Dedicated to Kim Cemer

The Birth of Jesus

was coming toward them, they took off! The enemy fled that day from the Lord's army.

David was the greatest king of Israel, a man after God's own heart. God took David from the pasture and made him the ruler over His people. Many kings came after David, but none ruled like David did.

God made a covenant with David, promising that through his family, the King of kings would come. The new King would be born in the City of David and many signs would confirm who He was.

He would answer the cry for help coming from the nation of Israel. Israel desired to be saved from the hand of their enemies. They wanted to serve God without fear, in holiness and righteousness all their days.

The King would be born of a virgin woman. His name would be Emmanuel, which means God with us. He would come from heaven and would be a horn of salvation. The promised King would reign wisely and do all that is just and right. He would be the Lord, our righteousness.

The Father told me a story about the birth of a child who would save my life. He talked about a promise He made long ago: from the womb of a woman, a Savior would be born. As I sat and listened, He went on to explain.

There was a young woman named Mary, and an angel appeared to her saying, "Rejoice, highly favored one. Do not be afraid for you have found favor with God, and you shall conceive in your womb, bring forth a Son, and call His name Jesus. He is the son of God."

This was all done that it might be fulfilled, which was spoken by the prophet saying, "Behold, the virgin shall be with child, and bring forth a Son, and you will call His name, Emmanuel, which means *God with us*."

Just as the prophecy was given long ago, Jesus was born of Mary in the town of Bethlehem. They wrapped Him in strips of cloth and laid Him in a manger. In the fields close by, shepherds were keeping watch over their sheep that night. An angel of the Lord appeared, and the glory of the Lord shined around them.

The angel said, "Do not be afraid, for I bring good news of joy; for there is born to you today a Savior, who is Christ the Lord. This will be a sign to you. You will find the baby wrapped in strips of cloth and lying in a manger."

Then there appeared with the angel a multitude of the heavenly host praising God and saying, "Glory to God in the Highest, and on earth, peace, goodwill to men."

"The Birth of Jesus" by Alicia Steiner, 9 years old (2008)
New Life Tabernacle Homer, AK

The angels departed, and the shepherds said to each other, "Let us go to Bethlehem to find the baby the angel told us about." They went and found Mary, Joseph, and the baby. The baby was wrapped in strips of cloth, lying in a manger, just as the angel said! The shepherds shared with Mary and Joseph what the angel had told them. Mary kept all these things in her heart concerning her baby, Jesus.

After Jesus was born, wise men came from the East to Jerusalem saying, "Where is He who has been born, King of the Jews? For we have seen His star and have come to worship Him."

Jesus was not in Jerusalem, for, as the prophet Micah wrote, "He will come from the land of Judah, in a town called Bethlehem." So, the wise men departed and went on to Bethlehem hoping to find Him there.

The star went before them and stood over where the young child lived. When the wise men saw the star, they rejoiced to have found the child! When they came into the house, they saw young Jesus with Mary, His mother. They bowed down and worshipped Him. They brought treasures with them to give to the child. They brought gifts of gold, frankincense, and myrrh. Then, they departed, happy in their hearts to have found the young King of the Jews.

"Dear God," I asked, "Why do I need this Son I have been given?"

He answered, "Sin entered into the world and brought darkness with it. The Son is the light of the world, and He offers life to men. So, whoever walks in His light will have no darkness in him."

As I thought about the story of the birth of Jesus, I was amazed! He was born just like I was, and yet, He was so very different. He came to the world that was dark and full of sin to shine a light of hope and save people from their sins. He was born to be a Savior, a Ruler, and a King. He even had His own star to show His Majesty.

Jesus' Baptism & Ministry

As Jesus grew, He became strong and was filled with wisdom. The grace of God was upon Him. He grew up as a carpenter's son in the town of Nazareth. At age thirty, Jesus left His home and went to the Jordan River where He found John the Baptist, His cousin. John dressed in camel's hair and had a leather belt around his waist. He ate locust and wild honey.

God sent John to preach in the wilderness. John lifted his voice and cried, "Prepare the way of the Lord; make straight a highway for our God."

John preached the baptism of repentance and said to the people, "There is One who is coming who is mightier than I. I baptize with water, but He will baptize with the Holy Ghost and fire."

When John saw Jesus coming, he said, "Behold, the Lamb of God who takes away the sin of the world! This is the One I spoke about; the One I said would come."

At Jesus' request, John baptized Him in the Jordan River. John testified, "I saw the Spirit descending from heaven like a dove, and it stayed upon Him. He is the One who will baptize with the Holy Ghost and fire."

After Jesus' baptism, He went out and began preaching. "The time is fulfilled, and the kingdom of God is at hand. Repent and believe the gospel."

He also called disciples to follow Him. At the Sea of Galilee, Jesus called to fishermen, "Follow me, and I will make you fishers of men." He chose twelve disciples in all: Simon Peter, Andrew, James and his brother John, Philip, Thomas, Matthew, James the son of Alphaeus, Simon, Jude, Judas Iscariot, and Bartholomew. Jesus called them to follow Him and preach the gospel. He empowered them to pray for the sick to be healed and to cast out the devils in His name.

"John the Baptist"
Madeleine Steiner, 9 years old
Landmark Tabernacle, Denver, CO

Jesus traveled through Galilee, teaching and preaching. He told the people, "You are the light of the world. Do not let your light be hidden, and don't let Satan blow it out. Let it shine before men, so they can see your good works and glorify your Father, which is in Heaven. Whoever comes to Me and hears My sayings and does them is like a wise man who builds his house on a rock. When the rains come and the winds blow, the house on the rock will stand firm. But whoever hears My sayings and doesn't do them, will be like a foolish man who builds his house on the sand. When the rains come and the winds blow, the house on the sand will fall flat!"

As people heard of Jesus' fame, they brought the sick and lame wherever He was. He healed all kinds of diseases. He made the lame walk, the blind see, the deaf hear, and even raised the dead to life again! People would come close to Him, begging to touch even the hem of his garment. As many who touched it, He healed and made well!

"House on the Rock"
Gage Carter, 12 years old
Zion Tabernacle, Kokomo, IN
Dedicated to Bro. & Sis. David Mathis

Once, Jesus was preaching in a house. Many people came to hear his teaching. So many people came they filled the room. Four men wanted to bring a paralyzed man to Jesus for healing, but they couldn't get in the door. Instead, they climbed onto the roof of the house and tore through the roof! Then, they lowered the man in his bed right in front of Jesus.

Jesus saw the faith of the men and told the man in the bed, "Son, your sins are forgiven. Arise! Take up your bed and walk!"

The man walked out of the house, and people were amazed! They glorified God saying, "We have never seen anything like this!"

One day, Jesus was tired and wanted to be alone, so He sent his disciples in a boat to the other side of the Sea of Galilee. He sent the multitudes away and went to the mountain to pray. When it was evening, Jesus saw a mighty wind tossing the boat where the disciples were. Jesus went to them, walking on the sea. The disciples saw Him coming and were afraid.

They cried, "It is a ghost!"

Jesus spoke to them, "It is I. Do not be afraid!"

"Take Your Friend to Jesus"
Jonathan Burner, 13 years old
Apostolics of Salem, Illinois

Peter answered Jesus, "Lord, if it's You, let me come to You on the water."

Jesus told him to come, so Peter climbed out of the boat and walked on the water, but then Peter looked down at the raging sea. He was afraid and began to sink.

"Lord save me!" He cried out.

Jesus stretched out His hand to catch him and said, "You of little faith, why did you doubt?" When they climbed into the boat, the wind stopped, and the sea was calm. The disciples came to Jesus and worshipped Him saying, "Truly, You are the Son of God."

"Jesus and Peter Walking on the Water"
Caden Gilliam, 11 years old
Christina Gilliam, 10 years old
Grace Point Church, Blairsville, GA

One day, while He was out traveling and preaching, Jesus got word from His friend Lazarus' sisters saying their brother was sick. Jesus loved Lazarus and his sisters, Mary and Martha. When Jesus heard Lazarus was sick, He said, "This sickness is not unto death, but for the glory of God, that the Son of God may be glorified through it."

He waited for two days, then Jesus said it was time to go to Bethany, where Lazarus was. Jesus told the disciples, "Our friend Lazarus sleeps, but I go that I may wake him up."

The disciples thought Lazarus was really asleep. Maybe he needed his rest to get better.

Jesus spoke more plainly to them and said, "Lazarus is dead."

When Jesus got there, He found out Lazarus had been in the tomb for four days. Martha ran to Jesus, when she heard He was there, and said, "Lord, if You had been here, my brother would not have died."

Jesus told Martha, "Your brother will rise again. I am the resurrection and the life." Mary also came to where Jesus was, weeping. Jesus said, "Where have you laid him?" They brought Jesus to the tomb and Jesus wept.

Some of the Jews that were there said, "See how He loved him!"

Others said, "Could not this Man, who opened the eyes of the blind, also have kept Lazarus from dying?"

Jesus went to the tomb. It was a cave with a stone lying against the opening, and Jesus said, "Take away the stone."

"Lazarus has been in the tomb four days," Martha said to Jesus, "Lord, by now, he stinks."

Jesus told Martha, "If you believe, you will see the glory of God."

When they removed the stone, Jesus lifted His eyes to heaven and prayed. When He was done praying, He cried with a loud voice, "Lazarus! Come forth!"

To their amazement, Lazarus came out. He was wrapped in grave clothes, and his face was covered. Jesus said, "Loose him, and let him go."

"Lazarus" by Charity Brock, 10 years old
Living Waters Fellowship, Beaverton, OR

The Final Passover

It was time to celebrate Passover, and Jesus told Peter and John to go and prepare for a place for the disciples to have dinner together. Jesus wanted to eat the Passover meal with His disciples. He knew He was about to suffer at the hands of the chief priest and scribes.

Many people believed in Jesus, but there were certain Jewish religious leaders who wanted to kill Him. They didn't like how the Jewish people followed and believed in Jesus.

When the people heard that Jesus was coming to Jerusalem for the Passover feast, they took branches of palm trees and spread them out on the road. As Jesus came riding past them on a donkey, they cried out, "Hosanna! Blessed is He who comes in the name of the Lord! Hosanna in the highest! Peace in Heaven and glory in the highest to the King of Israel!"

Jesus told the people, "He who believes in me, believes not in me but in Him who sent me. He who sees me, sees Him who sent me. I have come as a light into the world, that whoever believes in Me should not stay in darkness."

That evening, as Jesus and His disciples were eating their Passover meal, Jesus took some bread, blessed it, broke it, and passed it around the table.

"Take and eat. This is My body."

Then, He took the cup, gave thanks, and gave it to them saying, "Drink from it, all of you. This is My blood of the new covenant, which is shed for the remission of all sins."

Jesus told the disciples not to let their hearts be troubled. He told them if they believed in God, they should also believe in Him. Jesus said He was going away, to his Father's house, to prepare a place for them, but that He would return and bring them to that place He would prepare.

"You know the way to the place where I am going," Jesus said.

Thomas replied they didn't know the place, so they didn't know how to get there.

"I am the Way, the Truth, and the Life. No one comes to the Father except through Me," Jesus replied. "If you really knew Me, you would know My Father as well. From now on, you do know Him and have seen Him."

Philip said, "Lord, show us the Father and that will be enough for us."

Jesus answered, "Don't you know me, Philip, even after I have been among you such a long time? Anyone who has seen me has seen the Father. How can you

"Triumphal Entry" by Amelia Bowers, 11 years old
Lincoln, NE, Dedicated to Marc and Teresa Shoemaker

The Crucifixion

say, 'Show us the Father? Don't you believe that I am in the Father, and that the Father is in me? The words I say to you are not my own. Rather, it is the Father, living in me, who is doing His work."

While Jesus was with His disciples, He was preparing them for what would take place that night. He was preparing them for His departure. Jesus spent time talking to them about a Comforter that would come to them and live in them forever. "I will not leave you comfortless. I will come to you," He said. He spoke of the Spirit of Truth, whom the world knew nothing about.

The next story God told is very sad. It's about Jesus and how He died. It made me sad to hear it, but the story doesn't end here! In the middle of the story, I had to stop and ask God some questions.

After eating their Passover meal, Jesus and His disciples went to a garden. Jesus wanted to pray, but the disciples were tired and fell asleep. Jesus prayed anyway. He knew what was about to happen, and He needed strength to go forward.

A group of men, led by Judas, one of Jesus' disciples, found Him in the garden. They arrested Jesus and took Him before the high priest for questioning. They decided Jesus was guilty of blasphemy and sent him to Pontius Pilate, the Roman ruler of the land, for punishment.

Pilate asked Jesus, "Are you the King of the Jews?"

Jesus replied, "My kingdom is not of this world, but you are right in calling Me a King. It was why I was born and came into the world. Anyone that will hear My voice will believe it."

Pilate couldn't find any fault with Jesus, so he asked the Jewish people if they wanted him to release Jesus, or a prisoner named Barabbas who was a murderer and thief.

The crowd cried, "Barabbas! Give us Barabbas."

Pilate told the guards to whip Jesus. The soldiers put a crown of thorns on His head, a purple robe on His beaten and bloody back, and a reed in His right hand. Each one of them bowed a knee before Jesus and mocked Him, saying, "Hail, King of the Jews!" They spit on Him and hit Him.

Pilate brought Jesus back out in front of the crowd, wearing the crown of thorns and the purple robe. Pilate told the people, "Behold the man!"

"Calvary" by Temperance Leffler, 8 years old
New Life Tabernacle, Homer, AK

When the chief priests and officers saw Jesus, they shouted, "Crucify Him, crucify Him!"

Pilate knew Jesus was not guilty or worthy to be put to death, so he said to them, "Shall I crucify your King?"

The people cried out, "We have no king but Caesar!"

Afraid of the crowd, but unwilling to take responsibility for Jesus' death, Pilot washed his hands and told the people that Jesus' blood was on their heads. He gave Jesus to the people, and they led Him away to be crucified.

They took Jesus to Golgotha, a hill of death, where He would hang on a cross to die a slow and painful death. The cross Jesus carried was too heavy for Him, and He fell under the weight of it, so the soldiers ordered a man named Simon to carry the cross for Jesus.

Once they reached the peak of the hill, the soldiers nailed Jesus to the cross and hung Him in between two criminals. They wrote an inscription and put it above His head. It said, "This is Jesus the Nazarene, the King of the Jews."

Then Jesus said, "Father, forgive them, for they do not know what they do."

Jesus was thirsty and someone gave Him sour wine. Then He said, "It is finished!" He bowed His head and died.

When the soldiers saw Him, they wanted to make sure he was dead, so they pierced His side with a spear, and blood and water came out. After that, a disciple of Jesus, named Joseph, asked Pilate for Jesus' body. A man named Nicodemus brought a mixture of myrrh and aloes to put on Jesus' body. They took Him and wrapped Him in clean linen cloth filled with the spices. Joseph laid Jesus in a brand-new tomb, which was cut out of a large rock. Guards rolled a large stone over the opening.

At this point in the story, I was overwhelmed and confused. I needed to stop and ask God some questions.

"Father," I asked, "Why would anyone want to kill Jesus? He was a good man and he didn't hurt anyone. The Jews let a bad person go free and picked Jesus to die. He healed the sick, raised the dead, and opened blind eyes. He fed multitudes of people. He taught people to love You and to treat others like they would want to be treated. At Jesus' birth, the wise men said He was a king. He even had His own star to prove it."

The Father patiently explained to me how the prophets of old spoke of Jesus' birth and those prophecies came to pass, but they also spoke of His death. Isaiah spoke of One who would suffer at the hands of men for the sins of man.

"Jesus is the suffering Servant. He was despised and rejected by men. He felt sorrow and grief, and He alone is able to comfort those who experience grief and sorrow. He was wounded for our transgressions and bruised for our iniquities. The punishment that brought us peace was upon Him and, by His wounds, we are healed."

The Father reminded me of how Jesus was whipped, spit upon, and slapped. He explained that had to happen for the healing of mankind.

He reminded me that when John the Baptist saw Jesus coming, he said, "Behold the Lamb of God who takes away the sins of the world." Jesus is the Lamb who was taken to be slaughtered as a perfect and sinless sacrifice.

He was willing to die because He loved us. He didn't even open His mouth to defend Himself. He offered His soul and His body for the sins of man. The Servant who would justify many bore the sin of us all. Jesus loved the world and was willing to die, so that we all might have Life through His name.

And now, for the rest of the story . . .

"He is Risen" by Beckett Fuqua, 9 years old
Calvary Tabernacle, Quincy, IL
Dedicated to Sis. Annita Wasmundt

Resurrection

The Father spoke to me of how Jesus is the Savior of the world. He reminded me of the story of when the angel appeared to Joseph. Remember, the angel told Joseph to name the child Jesus because He would save His people from their sins. The angels told the shepherds a Savior was born, Christ the Lord.

The name *Jesus* means Jehovah is the Savior, our salvation. The praises that the children gave to Jesus in the temple were the same words people said to Jesus when he was riding on the donkey. Those were words of prophecy from Psalms 118, "O Lord save us! Blessed is He who comes in the name of the Lord; the Lord is God, and He has made His light shine upon us."

All people have sinned against God. We need a Savior to save us from our sins. The darkness of sin separated us from God, but He made a way, through Jesus, to bring the world back to Himself.

Jesus is the Light of the world. John the Baptist preached about One who was coming, and he called Him the true Light. The Light that gives light to every man came in the world. Jesus, on behalf of the world, paid the price for all sin. Because Jesus suffered for the world, the Light of Life can dwell in whoever believes in Him.

The story of Jesus did not end at His death and burial. Jesus couldn't stay in the grave if He was going to save men from their sin. His death was a part of our salvation, but so is His resurrection.

Remember when Jesus was in Jerusalem, He went to the temple and drove out the money changers? The Jewish leaders wanted a sign from Jesus to show them who gave Him authority to do what He did.

Jesus told them, "Destroy this temple, and in three days I will raise it up."

The Jews replied to Jesus, saying, "It took forty-six years to build the temple! It would be impossible to rebuild it in three days."

What they didn't know was Jesus wasn't speaking of the temple building, but of His body. Jesus would die, but He also would rise again in three days.

After Jesus was put into the tomb, Mary Magdalene and James' mother came to the tomb, bringing spices to anoint Jesus' body. They came very early, wondering how they were going to roll the stone away to anoint the body of Jesus.

There was a great earthquake as an angel of the Lord came from heaven and rolled away the stone. The angel's appearance was like lightning, and his clothes were as white as snow. The guards that were watching Jesus' tomb were so afraid they couldn't move.

The women entered the tomb but did not find the body of the Lord Jesus. As they turned, they saw the angel of the Lord. The women were afraid and bowed their faces to the ground.

The angel said to them, "Why do you seek the living among the dead? He is not here but is risen! Come see the place where the Lord did lay."

As the angel spoke, the women remembered what Jesus had said to them when He was in Galilee. He had told them, "The Son of Man must be delivered into the hands of sinful men, be crucified, and the third day rise again."

The angel told them to go back to Galilee for Jesus would meet them there. They ran as fast as they could in awe and full of great joy to tell the disciples all they had seen and heard.

Jesus appeared to His disciples, and to certain men and women after He rose from the dead. Thomas, one of the disciples, wasn't present when Jesus appeared to the other disciples. The others told Thomas, "We have seen the Lord!"

Thomas replied, "Unless I see the nail marks in His hands, and put my finger where the nails were, and put my hand into His side, I will not believe."

The next time Jesus appeared in the midst of the disciples, Thomas was there.

Jesus looked at Thomas and said, "Put your finger here; see my hands. Reach out your hand and put it into my side. Stop doubting and believe."

When Thomas saw Jesus, His nail scarred hands and side, he said, "My Lord and My God."

Jesus acknowledged that Thomas believed because of what he saw, but He said blessed are those who haven't seen, yet still believe.

Jesus did many miracles in the presence of the disciples. Some of the miracles were written down so the world may believe that Jesus is the Christ, the Son of the living God. Whoever believes will have life in His name.

Jesus told the disciples if they believed in God, they needed to believe in Him also. The world is separated from God because of sin. God is life, and that same life is in Jesus Christ. Jesus rose from the dead, so we can, through him, have eternal life. It is in Jesus that we have hope in this life and in eternity.

Remember during His ministry, Jesus once asked a Samaritan woman for a drink of water. The woman was surprised that Jesus, being a Jew, would ask a half-Jew for a drink. Jesus told the woman if she knew the gift of God, and who it was she was talking to, she would ask

Him for a drink, and He would give her living water so she would never thirst again. He told her the water in the well would only make her thirsty and leave her wanting more, but the water He gives would become a fountain of water springing up into everlasting life.

Jesus stayed with the disciples and others He chose to show Himself alive to for forty days after He resurrected. He taught them of the things concerning the kingdom of God. Jesus commissioned his disciples to further his ministry. He said to them, "This is what I told you while I was still with you: Everything must be fulfilled that is written about me in the Law of Moses, the Prophets, and the Psalms."

Jesus opened their minds so they could understand the Scriptures. He told them what was written about Himself. He said it was necessary for Him to suffer and rise from the dead on the third day. And repentance for the remission of sins would be preached in His name, to all nations, beginning at Jerusalem. Jesus told the disciples to go into the whole world and preach the gospel.

The gospel is the good news of Jesus Christ, his death, burial, and resurrection. Jesus said whoever believes and is baptized will be saved; but he who doesn't believe is condemned already. Jesus said signs would follow those who believe. In His name they will cast out demons and speak in new tongues. In His name, they will pick up snakes with their hands and not be harmed. In His name, if they were to drink deadly poison, it will not hurt them. In His name, when they lay hands on the sick, they will recover. Jesus told the disciples they would witnesses these things.

Jesus said to the disciples, "All authority in heaven and on earth has been given to me. Therefore, go and make disciples of all nations, baptizing them in the name of the Father and of the Son and of the Holy Spirit, and teaching them to obey everything I have commanded you. And surely, I am with you always, to the very end of the age."

Jesus said to them, "Behold, I send the promise of My Father upon you, but tarry in the city of Jerusalem until you are endued with power from on high." Jesus told the disciples not to leave Jerusalem but to wait for the promise He spoke to them about. He said, "For John truly baptized with water, but you shall be baptized with the Holy Spirit not many days from now. You shall receive power when the Holy Spirit has come upon you; and you shall be witnesses to me in Jerusalem, and in all Judea and Samaria, and to the end of the earth."

Jesus promised them that He would never leave them nor forsake them. He told them He would be with them always to the end of the world. Jesus would give them power to do the things He commissioned and sent them to do. Jesus said He would come to them, and He kept that promise in the Holy Spirit.

Remember, before He died while they were eating the Passover meal together, Jesus told the disciples He had to go away to prepare a place for them, and so He could send the Comforter—the Holy Spirit—to them. The disciples believed what Jesus said. They witnessed that He rose from the dead, and they were about to experience the promise of God in their lives, and in the lives of others.

After Jesus finished teaching them, He lifted up His hands and blessed them. He promised to return for them in person to take them to Heaven to be with Him forever. They watched him ascend up into Heaven from Mount Olivet, near Jerusalem. The disciples looked steadfastly toward Heaven as Jesus went up.

Then, two angels appeared in white clothing and said to them, "Men of Galilee, why do you stand gazing into Heaven? This same Jesus, who was taken up from you, will so come in like manner as you saw Him go to Heaven."

They worshipped the Lord and returned to Jerusalem with great joy to wait for the promise of the Holy Spirit. Jesus lived on earth with His followers for three and a half years, but He was about to live in them through the Holy Spirit.

"Ascension" by Julian Bowers, 9 years old, Lincoln, NE
Dedicated to Robert & Barbara Herrington

The Promise Fulfilled

When they went to Jerusalem from Mount Olivet, they went to an upper room to wait for the promised Comforter. There were 120 people gathered, including the eleven disciples, some women, Mary the mother of Jesus, and His brothers. They were praying with a united spirit, waiting for the promise Jesus spoke to them about.

It was fifty days after Passover, the Day of Pentecost. Pentecost was a celebration of harvest where people brought their first fruits to God. As the believers were gathered in the upper room, suddenly there came a sound from Heaven. It sounded like the blowing of a mighty wind, and it filled the whole room where they were sitting.

Then they saw what seemed to be tongues of fire, and it separated and sat on each one of them. They were all filled with the Holy Spirit and began to speak in other tongues as the Spirit spoke through them. The Spirit gave them the ability to speak in other languages they didn't know how to speak. Jesus told them they would speak in new tongues, and He told them the Holy Spirit would bring to their remembrance all the things He had ever told them. They were witnesses of the promise, and what Jesus said would happen came to pass.

At the same time as the meeting in the upper room, there were other God fearing-Jews in Jerusalem to celebrate Pentecost, the feast of weeks. These Jews had gathered from every nation under heaven for the harvest celebration. The visitors to Jerusalem heard the sound of the people in the upper room speaking in their languages. They were amazed because the men and women were Galileans and not from where they lived.

They said, "We hear them speaking in our own tongues the wonderful works of God." The people in Jerusalem were amazed, and some thought the believers were drunk. Peter stood up and explained that they weren't drunk, but what was happening to them was a fulfillment of scripture.

He said, "This is what was spoken by the prophet Joel: 'In the last days, God said, I will pour out my Spirit on all people. Your sons and daughters will prophesy, your young men will see visions, your old men will dream dreams. On my servants, both men and women, I will pour out my Spirit in those days, and they will prophesy.'"

Peter went on to tell them about Jesus of Nazareth, and the miracles, wonders, and signs that God did through Him in their midst. He preached about how it was the plan of God that Jesus die for the sins of mankind. He said that they, along with the help of wicked men, put Jesus to death by nailing Him to the cross. But God

"Pentecost" by Leah Elkins, 14 years old
Mt. Zion UPC, Hosford, FL

-Leah

raised Him from the dead, freeing Him from the agony of death, because it was impossible for death to keep its hold on Him!

God raised Jesus to life, and they, the 120 in the upper room, were all witnesses of it. Jesus was exalted to the right hand of God. Jesus poured out the promised Holy Spirit, and that is what they saw and heard. All Israel could be assured of this: God made Jesus, whom they crucified, both Lord and Messiah!

When the people heard this, they were cut to the heart and said to Peter and the other apostles, "Brothers, what shall we do?"

Peter answered, "Repent, and let every one of you be baptized in the name of Jesus Christ for the remission of sins, and you shall receive the gift of the Holy Spirit. For the promise is to you and to your children, and to all who are afar off, as many as the Lord our God shall call."

Remember when John the Baptist was preaching and baptizing? He told the people there was One coming who would baptize them with the Holy Spirit and fire. What the crowd heard and saw that day was Jesus baptizing with the Holy Spirit and tongues of fire. Peter told the people that the gift of the Holy Spirit was also for them.

Remember when I told you a man named Nicodemus helped Joseph with the burial of Jesus? Nicodemus was a Pharisee, a ruler of the Jews. Long before Jesus' death and resurrection, Nicodemus came to Jesus secretly at night to ask Him questions.

Nicodemus said, "Rabbi, we know that You are a teacher that comes from God; for no one can do these signs that You do unless God is with him."

Jesus spoke to Nicodemus about a second birth that would happen, and it would be different then a human birth. The second birth is from above, and it's a birth of water and Spirit. If one is to see the kingdom of God, then he has to be born again.

Jesus said, "Most assuredly, I say to you, unless one is born again, he cannot see the kingdom of God."

Nicodemus asked, "How can a man be born when he is old? Can he enter a second time into his mother's womb and be born?"

Jesus answered, "Most assuredly, I say to you, unless one is born of water and the Spirit, he cannot enter the kingdom of God. That which is born of the flesh is flesh, and that which is born of the Spirit is spirit. Do not marvel that I said to you, 'You must be born again.' The wind blows where it wishes, and you hear the sound of it, but cannot tell where it comes from and where it goes. So is everyone who is born of the Spirit."

Peter told the Jews on the Day of Pentecost about the new birth that Jesus told Nicodemus about. What Jesus said to Nicodemus about the wind was just like what happened in the upper room. Remember, when the 120 were filled with the Spirit? It came in like a mighty wind and filled them! They spoke with tongues, and that was the sound the people heard. Everyone that receives the Spirit experiences it just like the 120 did at Pentecost. Everyone who believes is also baptized with water in Jesus' name.

Jesus had told the disciples that repentance and remission of sins should be preached in His name to all nations, beginning at Jerusalem. Peter didn't have to think about the message he was going to preach to those people that day, because it was the Holy Spirit who gave him the words to say. Peter had the Holy Spirit and the power he needed to be a witness and preach Jesus to the people.

That day, three thousand people believed and were baptized! God has been adding to His church daily since that day!

"Baptism" by Noah Schlupp, 11 years old
The Rock Church, Pearl City, HI

Baptism

"Dear Father," I asked, "there was something Jesus said that doesn't quite make sense to me. Jesus told the disciples to baptize in the name of the Father, and of the Son, and of the Holy Spirit. Did they do that? You said Peter stood up and told the people to be baptized in Jesus' name."

The Father was so kind in answering my question. He reminded me of the promise spoken by Isaiah the prophet, "For unto us a child is born, unto us a Son is given; And the government will be upon His shoulder. And His name will be called Wonderful, Counselor, Mighty God, Everlasting Father, Prince of Peace." He also reminded me of when Jesus said, "If you have seen me, you have seen the Father. I and my Father are one!"

The simple answer to your question is, "Yes! Baptizing in Jesus' name is exactly what the disciples were supposed to do to obey Jesus. Jesus is the name of the Father, Son, and Holy Spirit! He is the Mighty God, Everlasting Father, and the Comforter!"

He explained it again, in more detail. Isaiah spoke of a Son who would be born for the world. Isaiah didn't give us His human name but did give us a list of distinguishing traits and qualities He is marked with. "For unto us a child is born, unto us a Son is given; And the government will be upon His shoulder. And His name will be called Wonderful, Counselor, Mighty God, Everlasting Father, Prince of Peace." We know Him by these characteristics.

Jesus is wonderful. Jesus did many marvelous works when He was on earth and still does today. Jesus is a wonderful Savior.

Jesus is the Counselor. Jesus told the disciples they didn't need to worry about how they were going to defend themselves because He would give them words and wisdom that none of their adversaries would be able to resist or contradict. If you need anything, Jesus is the one to help.

Jesus is Mighty God. Jesus is God with us. That's what an angel told Joseph in a dream. He is the all powerful God, not just a powerful man. Remember when Thomas saw Jesus for the first time after He arose from the dead, and what he said? He said, "My Lord and My God!"

Jesus is the Everlasting Father. Everlasting is without beginning or end, and Father is one who brings things into existence. That sounds like God! God created the heaven and the earth, the first parents, and me. He has always been, and that is who Jesus is!

Jesus is the Prince of Peace. A prince is a founder, author, leader, lord, and ruler. Peace is freedom from trouble, freedom from bondage, and a change of attitude on the part of two individuals. Remember when the angels praised God and said, "Glory to God in the highest, and on earth peace to men on whom His favor rests?" They cried "Peace!" because there would finally be peace between God and man. The world would be reconciled to God because of the Son of God. The Lord is the Spirit and where the Spirit of the Lord is there is freedom.

So, let us put it all together. Jesus was a man born like us, but He has a name that describes Him differently. He was human in the sense that He was born of a woman. That's why we call Him the son of man. Jesus was born of the Holy Spirit, so that also makes Him the Son of God.

Jesus is God in every way. He is the creator of all things and has no beginning or end. He is the one true God—there's only one God. He's the advisor who leads and guides into all truth. Think about how he led Peter on the day of Pentecost when he stood up and preached. Peter didn't have to think about what he was going to say because Jesus gave him the words and the wisdom needed to speak to the hearts of the people.

Remember when Jesus talked about sending a Comforter to the disciples, and later said the Comforter is the Holy Spirit? Well that word Comforter means Counselor.

A counselor is someone who comforts people who are grieving and sorrowful. The word Comforter means intercessor and advocate. He is one who pleads on the behalf of someone else, to reconcile one to another.

Remember when I told you that Isaiah the prophet spoke of Jesus' death? Jesus bore the weight of the world's sin and carried its grief and sorrow. In dying on the cross, He was our Comforter.

He also intercedes for men, so they could be reconciled to God because they are enemies of God. Jesus died a sinner's death, but He was sinless. He let the sinful, guilty ones go free. Jesus paid the price; His soul was an offering for sin. Jesus is the Comforter, who is the Holy Spirit.

I thought about these words and this child given. It was for me He came, and the promise given.

So, to answer the question about baptism, what Peter said was true! Baptism has to be done in Jesus' name. Peter was doing what Jesus commanded because Jesus is the Father, Son, and Holy Ghost. Jesus told Philip, "When you see me you see the Father. The Father is in me and I in Him." Jesus said if they would abide in His word, they would be His disciples, and they would know the truth, and the truth would make them free.

Remember when Jesus told the Jews, "You are from beneath; I am from above. You are of this world; I am not of this world. Therefore, I say to you that if you do not believe that I am He, you will die in your sins?" Unless they believed that Jesus was their God and Father, they would die in their sins.

The Jews who were in Jerusalem on the day of Pentecost feared God. They were there celebrating a festival that was commanded in the Old Testament. What Peter preached that day was different than what they believed. Peter preached Jesus because they had to believe in Him to find salvation, or they would die in their sins.

Peter told the people to repent and to be baptized in Jesus' name for the remission of sins, and they would receive the gift of the Holy Spirit. This promise wasn't just for them but for their children and for all generations to come. It was for the whole world. Peter warned them to save themselves from their corrupt generation. Those who accepted Peter's message that day were baptized, and three thousand souls were saved by the good news, or gospel, of Jesus' death, burial, and resurrection.

Jesus said salvation would start in Jerusalem and spread from there to the ends of the earth. We see how salvation began in Jerusalem on the day of Pentecost. Salvation comes through Jesus, His death, burial, and resurrection. Salvation is found in no one else, for there is no other name under heaven given to men by whom they must be saved.

Salvation comes through both water birth and Spirit birth. Believers must put on Christ through baptism and repentance of sin. They must obey the gospel—the good news of Jesus' death, burial, and resurrection.

Jesus' flesh and blood, His humanity, was crucified for the world. Believers crucify their flesh when they repent. They are buried with Christ when they are baptized in Jesus' name.

Then Jesus rose from the dead! Believers receive the Holy Spirit as they are raised to walk in new life. The Gospel of Jesus truly is the world's hope of glory!

Wow! I just want to celebrate Jesus!

"Share the Gospel" by Natalie Schlupp, 11 years old
The Rock Church, Pearl City, HI

And he said unto them, Go ye into all the world, and preach the gospel to every creature.

Mark 16:15

I Know His Name

The Father sat me on His knee and looked me in the eyes. He said, "Jesus was in the world and the world was made through Him, but the world did not know Him. He came to His own people, and they did not receive Him, but as many as received Jesus to them He gave the right to become the children of God because they believed in His name: the children were not born from human parents, but of God."

Jesus came in God's likeness and character. He is the exact image of God in the flesh. God was in Jesus reconciling the world unto Himself. Jesus is the image of the invisible God, who promised to redeem His people and save them from their sins.

God is a Spirit, and they that worship God must worship Him in Spirit and in truth. Jesus is the way, the truth, and the life. In order for man to worship God the way He wants them to, they have to believe in Jesus. Jesus is God's plan of salvation for the world.

Salvation was for the Jews first. Zacharias prophesied, "Blessed is the Lord God of Israel! For He has visited and redeemed His people and has raised up a horn of salvation for us in the house of His servant David." Jesus—the Savior—was also given to the Gentiles. Isaiah wrote, "I will also give You as a light to the Gentiles, that You should be My salvation to the ends of the earth."

God is the Father, Savior, and Redeemer. He said, "Look unto Me, and be ye saved, all the ends of the earth; for I am God and there is none else."

In Jesus dwells all the fullness of God, and mankind is complete in Him. Jesus is the one true God. The world is to serve God only and love Him only and to be taught of Him only. When the world serves Jesus, they are serving God. When we believe in Jesus, we believe He is God with us. Jesus is the new covenant and fulfillment of the old covenant. Behold all things have become new!

I looked into the Father's eyes and felt the warmth of His embrace. The words He spoke were the words of life. On the palms of His hands were the scars from the nails, which held Him nailed to the cross for the sins of the world. He created the world with all this in mind, and He calls us to come, and to eat of the bread, and to drink of the cup, which He gave for the life of the world.

Jesus is the Word made flesh. He dwelt among us and we beheld His glory, which is the glory of the Father full of grace and truth. If the gospel is hidden, it is hidden to those who are lost, whose minds the gods of this world have blinded, who do not believe. Those who are lost cannot see the light of the gospel of the glory of Christ, who is the image of God. For God commanded light to shine out of darkness, He made His light shine in our hearts to give us the light of the knowledge of the glory of God in the face of Jesus Christ.

The word of God warms my heart, and I hear Jesus calling me to come and drink of the water of life freely. I make my way to an altar of repentance asking Jesus to forgive me of my sins. I raise my hands and surrender my life to the One who died on the cross, who willingly spread out His hands, and took my sins and nailed them to His cross.

Just like the word of God said, I was baptized with the Holy Spirit and spoke in other tongues as the Spirit empowered me. God sent the Spirit of His Son into my heart as I called out, "Abba, Father."

I was baptized in the name of Jesus for the forgiveness of my sin. Now Jesus lives in me. My body is dead because of sin, but the Spirit is life because of righteousness. Jesus said, "I will not leave you fatherless; I will come to you."

"Prayer at the Altar" by Rachel Springer, 10 years old
East Gate UPC, Anchorage, AK

I'm in the LORD'S Army

I am a part of the family of God and have been given the family name. I am no longer a slave to sin, but a child of the King. I have been adopted into the family of God and possess all the rights as an heir. I have been given a new life. I know Jesus lives in my heart.

I have living hope through the resurrection of Jesus Christ from the dead. I have an inheritance that can never perish, spoil, or fade in Heaven for me. He said He will return for me the same way he left the earth. He will come back to take me to live with Him forever in the New Jerusalem.

As I sing the songs about Jesus, I now fully understand. I will let my light shine; I won't hide it or let it go out. I will hold my light high for the world to see that Jesus lives in me. I will be a wise man that builds a house on the rock, the winds will blow, and the rains will come, but I will stand firm on the foundation of God's word. I may never march, fight, or fly in the U. S. Military, but I will be a soldier in the Lord's army.

I will put on the whole armor of God and stand against the schemes of the devil. I will use the shield of faith to block the fiery darts that he shoots at me. I will use the sword of the Spirit, which is the word of God, and wear the helmet of salvation. I will wear the belt of truth buckled around my waist, the breastplate of righteousness, and have my feet fitted with the readiness that comes from the gospel of peace. I will be ready and stand my ground when the devil comes at me, and let the Lord fight my battle.

When we sing about father Abraham having many sons, I know that I am now one of them! I will sing from my heart and with my hands lifted high. From the rising of the sun to the going down of the same, the name of the Lord will be praised. Praise ye the Lord!

Celebrate Jesus!

"The Armor of God" by Jared Huffman, 14 years old
Life Tabernacle, Lincoln, NE
Dedicated to Bro. & Sis. Joe Huffman

Epilogue

When I celebrate Independence Day, remembering the birth of our nation, and the ones who gave their lives for the freedom we celebrate, I will always think of the freedom given to me on the cross of Calvary.

As the world shouted, "Crucify Him! Crucify Him!" God saw the light of salvation Jesus would give to a lost and dying world.

God saw the birth of a holy nation, a chosen people belonging to Him who would celebrate Him for bringing them out of darkness into His wonderful light. So, I will raise the blood-stained banner high and celebrate the new birth of Jesus Christ in my life!

Let the fireworks light up the sky and raise the flag of freedom up high! As the children of light, we are proud to say this is our Independence Day.

We will not forget the men who died defending our freedom, like Peter, Stephen, Paul, and others who gave their lives for the Gospel of Jesus Christ. They fought the good fight. They finished the race. They have kept the faith. There is laid up for them a crown of righteousness, which the righteous Judge will give to them in Heaven.

Like the ones who have passed on before me, I will defend and preach the gospel of Jesus Christ. It is the power of God for the salvation of everyone who believes!

"Soldiers and the Cross" by Colby Rathbun, 14 years old, Palm Coast, FL,
Dedicated to Rev. Stuart & Orvada Churchill, The Pentecostals of Palm Coast

A Note from the Author

I am honored and blessed to write again with my Lord and Savior Jesus Christ. He has given me the desire of my heart to write a children's book. I wanted to reflect on my own childhood life of Sunday school and church experiences that were so life-changing. Jesus said, "Let the little children come to me, and do not hinder them, for the kingdom of God belongs to such as these." I hope this book will help people of all ages celebrate the Word of life, Jesus Christ.

As I celebrate my 45th anniversary of rebirth in Christ, I can't help but to go back to the beginning and think about my life as a young child. I was five years old when we started going to the United Pentecostal Church on 26th and H St. in Lincoln, NE. That time was when life really started for me. I was nine years old when I was born of the water and the Spirit. I remember the alter that was upfront of the church. It was long and big to me, but it was at that altar that I traded death for life. Did I really understand the gift I had been given? No, but through the preaching and teaching of the Word and the Spirit of God living in me, I was put on a good path.

My heart is truly grateful to all the Sunday school teachers I had and the pastor I had growing up. I'm thankful for all the work that went into preparing sermons and Sunday school lessons, and for all the time spent on pictures and crafts to make Sunday school fun. They spent so much time and energy on Christmas programs, and getting us ready to participate. My favorite program was *The Christmas Carol*. We performed it as a church, and it was amazing! I remember all the prizes we earned for memory verses memorized, sword drills won, or bringing a friend to church, the list goes on. One prize in particular, which I still have, was a red Word Aflame Bible.

Brother Huffman, thank you for giving your Sunday school class airplane rides! It was my first flight! I remember all of the songs we learned: "This Little Light of Mine," "The Devil is a Sly O' Fox," "Father Abraham," "What Can Wash Away My Sins? Nothing but the Blood of Jesus," "Stop and Let Me Tell You What the Lord Has Done for Me," and "I'm in the Lord's Army." These are just a few of the songs I remember.

I want to thank my Mother for bringing her children to Jesus, so we could have eternal life. I always think of this song we learned in Sunday school: M is for the million things she gave me. O means that she's growing old. T is for the tears she shed to save me. H is for her heart of purest gold. E is for her eyes with love-light shining. And R means right she'll always be. Put them all together, they spell MOTHER, a word that means the world to me!

To Brother and Sister Andrew Wasmundt Sr. (Brother Wasmundt has gone on to meet the Lord), Sister Jeannie Crocker, Brother Joe and Sister Deloris Huffman, and Sister Annita Wasmundt—my pastor and teachers who had influence in my childhood—and numerous others who through the years have affected my life in some way, thank you from my heart. One other person that I would like to mention who was never my Sunday school teacher, but was still teaching a few years back, is Sister Connie McCarter. My heart was touched by your faithfulness to the lives of the children through all these years, thank you! My prayers and thoughts go out to all the teachers and ministers of Jesus Christ throughout the world, who will make a way for children to come to Jesus, for such is the kingdom of God!

Christine Steiner

steinerbooks.wordpress.com

Christine Steiner lives in Homer, Alaska. She is the author of Repentance to Life, *where she shares her testimony.*

You can contact her at christineleesteiner@gmail.com.

A Note from the Author's Mother

For my beautiful daughter, who has grown so much spiritually, for whom I give Jesus Christ all the glory. Christine asked me if I would write a little something about our experience in coming to Christ. I was 30 years old when I received the baptism of the Holy Ghost and was baptized in the beautiful name of Jesus Christ for the remission of sins—this all happened in 1970, the night before Mother's Day.

Through my life up until the time I received the Holy Ghost, I had been to at least seven different churches, and I always left empty in my heart. I needed help so badly, and I did not know where to turn. We had lived in Colorado for four years and one day I cried to God, "Oh, God help me! Somebody help me." It wasn't too long after that, my Mom paid our way back to Lincoln, NE.

It was there that a friend of mine, Joni Strom, invited us to a United Pentecostal Church. When my children and I walked through the doors of the church, I felt such a holiness I hadn't felt in any of the churches I had been to. You don't know what that meant to me.

I always knew in my heart that I wasn't right with God, but for the very first time I was told what I could do about it. I was given hope. Brother and Sister Andrew Wasmundt Sr. were pastoring the church at that time and they and the church people were so friendly. They made us feel welcome. They seemed so sincere, and I felt like they cared about my children and me. At that time, my husband and I had four children. In 1975, we had one more.

Brother and Sister Andrew Wasmundt Sr., Brother and Sister David Matthis, Brother and Sister Jones, Brother Joe and Sister Deloris Huffman, Sister Joni Strom, and Sister Jeannie Crocker, all had a part in bringing us to know and grow in Christ.

The night I received the Holy Ghost, it literally felt like someone had come along and was cutting off the chains that bound me. I was set free! When I was baptized in Jesus' Name, and I came up out of the watery grave, I found everything I needed. I didn't need to look anymore.

This is the way I must raise my children. I wanted so badly to be a better mother. I had made so many bad choices that affected my children. God was giving me another chance. Yes, there have been ups and downs since then, but Jesus is our Redeemer, Comforter, Peace, Strength, and Joy. He is all in all.

All five of our children have been baptized in Jesus' name, and four have received the Holy Ghost. I have been teaching the primary Sunday school class for close to 45 years. I always wanted to teach children to love and serve Jesus, so they wouldn't make the mistakes I made.

Jesus has always been so good to me and my family. To God be the glory!

Barbara Herrington

I lost a little friend today
She dawned her wings and flew away
She now plays where angels trod
And sleeps in the everlasting arms of God

*In remembrance of all the children
who have gone on to be with Jesus.*
Kathy Herrington

Fox Tales Children's Books

www.OurWrittenLives.com

www.ingramcontent.com/pod-product-compliance
Lightning Source LLC
Chambersburg PA
CBHW042111090526
44592CB00005B/87